IMAGES
of America

ARIZONA'S NATIONAL
PARKS AND MONUMENTS

A FREE GOVERNMENT SERVICE
GRAND CANYON
NATIONAL PARK
U.S. DEPARTMENT OF THE INTERIOR
NATIONAL PARK SERVICE

Arizona's incredible natural scenery and rich human heritage have long been the cornerstones of both Arizonans' sense of place and the face that they show to the rest of the world. The national parks and monuments of Arizona celebrate and preserve that natural scenery and human heritage and significantly contribute to Arizona's identity. (Courtesy of Library of Congress.)

ON THE COVER: Along with the Grand Canyon, few scenes are more iconic to the image of Arizona than this vista within Canyon de Chelly National Monument seen in the early part of the 20th century. Like many of the other national parks and monuments, Canyon de Chelly celebrates both Arizona's spectacular natural scenery and rich human heritage. (Courtesy of Library of Congress.)

IMAGES
of America

ARIZONA'S NATIONAL
PARKS AND MONUMENTS

Donna and George Hartz

ARCADIA
PUBLISHING

Published by Arcadia Publishing
Charleston, South Carolina

Printed in the United States of America

Library of Congress Control Number: 2013933151

For all general information, please contact Arcadia Publishing:
Telephone 843-853-2070
Fax 843-853-0044
E-mail sales@arcadiapublishing.com
For customer service and orders:
Toll-Free 1-888-313-2665

Visit us on the Internet at www.arcadiapublishing.com

*To those whose vision and perseverance protect these wondrous places
that speak to our spirits and our sense of place and connect us to
generations who came before and who will follow in our footsteps.*

CONTENTS

ACKNOWLEDGMENTS

Researching a book on national parks and monuments focuses you very quickly on the resources of the US federal government, and that is a very good thing. We discovered almost immediately a vast and extremely well-organized collection of historical information and photographs. This is something that our government has done very well, and it is a resource worth exploring even if you are not writing a book!

The National Park Service (NPS) maintains comprehensive websites for each of its national parks and monuments. The websites contain tourist information about each site, as well as sections on history, culture, nature, video and photography, and so on. Many of the individual sites contain links to online books about the history of the park or monument. For the more serious researcher, the NPS website contains links to huge databases of articles about the history and archaeology within the parks and monuments—full of fascinating information. In addition, the NPS maintains a website containing a portion of its historical photograph collection (www.nps.gov/hfc/cfm/npsphoto.cfm). It is easily searchable and contains thousands of great photographs. NPS also maintains a site (www.nps.gov/pub_aff/imagebase.html) containing many thousands more contemporary public domain photographs, which is again easily searchable. Additionally, from NPS, Grand Canyon and Petrified Forest maintain large and well-organized collections of photographs on Flickr. The Bureau of Land Management (BLM) also has websites for each of its national monuments, containing similar information to the NPS sites, including access to photographs. The BLM also maintains a large, searchable master website (www.blm.gov/wo/st/en/bpd.html) of its photograph collection. Finally, there are two other great sites for historical photographs. The Library of Congress has a fantastic site, well organized, and, again, easily searchable, with a huge collection of historical photographs (www.loc.gov/pictures). The US Geological Survey historical photograph collection is also a treasure trove (libraryphoto.cr.usgs.gov).

We also received a lot of help from real people. Many thanks go to the Scottsdale Public Library, Tempe Historical Society, Phoenix Zoo, Desert Botanical Garden, Friends of the Sonoran Desert National Monument, Kevin Wright and Bob Wick of BLM, and John Hervert of Arizona Game and Fish.

INTRODUCTION

On Saturday morning, June 9, 1906, the top headlines in the *Arizona Republican* newspaper were "Water Works Bonds Temporarily Tied Up" (by a lawsuit filed in Cincinnati alleging that Phoenix's city recorder failed to sign the paperwork) and "A Canadian Shaking Up" (about a cyclone raging through Ontario province). The *Chicago Daily Tribune*'s front page told its readers about "Packing Houses in True Light," "Thousands Hold Untaxed Wealth," and "Lone Women Tag Finicky Hotels" (about a business convention boycotting hotels that refused female guests after 6:00 p.m.). That same morning, the *New York Times* headlines included "Graft Question to All Pennsylvania Agents," "Called Woman out and Murdered Her," "King Edward Ignored The German Emperor," and "Facts In Meat Inquiry Satisfy The Committee." The only front page article on new legislation from Washington was a brief *New York Times* story headlined "Free Alcohol Bill Signed," a law exempting alcohol used in arts and industry from taxation as long as it was poisonous and unsafe to drink—apparently, important news that day. There was no mention in any of the papers on June 9 that Pres. Theodore Roosevelt had his mind on more than "free alcohol" the previous day; he had signed into law 16 USC 431-433, the American Antiquities Act of 1906. It went unreported that day, or any day at least through the following week, by these three prestigious newspapers. Sometimes it is hard to spot the really big stories, and the Antiquities Act of 1906 has proven to be of "monumental" importance for the United States and for Arizona. Some 140 of our national parks and monuments were preserved under this act, as well as 19 of the 20 national parks and monuments in Arizona. This legislation literally changed the face of Arizona.

Arizona's three national parks and 17 national monuments truly represent the face of the majesty of Arizona, as it is known around the world, and a huge part of the self-image of Arizonans. They preserve, celebrate, and make accessible much of what is unique about Arizona—from its magnificent Sonoran Desert and high-country flora to the mountains and canyons testifying to its amazing geologic history and to the extraordinary artifacts and creations of its earliest residents.

The history of the creation of Arizona's 20 national parks and monuments is a story of grassroots efforts by countless citizens, aided immensely by an extraordinary piece of Congressional legislation and aggressive actions by eight US presidents. The legislation was the American Antiquities Act of 1906, which allowed the president to unilaterally proclaim national monuments without the necessity of any Congressional action. The Antiquities Act has been used in Arizona more often than in any other state—a total of 23 times. Each of our three national parks (Grand Canyon, Petrified Forest, and Saguaro) was originally preserved as a national monument via the Antiquities Act. Two of the first four presidential proclamations were in Arizona (Montezuma Castle and Petrified Forest in December 1906), as well as five from January 2000 to January 2001.

In this book, we will tell the stories of the creation of each of Arizona's national parks and monuments, taking advantage of more than 200 historical photographs—with several more than 130 years old and many never before published.

In the first chapter, we review grassroots preservation efforts from the last decades of the 19th century to the early 20th century that led to the eventual passage of the Antiquities Act. We particularly focus on efforts to save Arizona's Casa Grande Ruins, whose deterioration provided major impetus to the preservation effort. The second chapter tells the story of Pres. Theodore Roosevelt's creation of the first national monuments in Arizona. Chapter three reviews in more detail the battle to protect and preserve the Grand Canyon—the uproar caused by Roosevelt's using the Antiquities Act to create the 800,000-plus-acre national monument that resulted in court battles and the eventual creation of Grand Canyon National Park. This amazing story is not widely known or appreciated. In chapter four, we showcase the creation of 13 more national monuments in Arizona during the next 90 years, particularly in the context of the creation and growth of the National Park Service. During this period, two of Arizona's national monuments (Petrified Forest and Saguaro) became national parks, and another (Marble Canyon) was absorbed into Grand Canyon National Park. Finally, in chapter five, we tell the story of the five huge Arizona national monuments proclaimed by Pres. Bill Clinton in 2000–2001, particularly his decision to have them administered by the Bureau of Land Management rather than the National Park Service.

The Antiquities Act of 1906 has been immensely important for Arizona and for all of the United States. It may not have been big news on June 9, 1906, probably because few at the editorial desks or even in Congress in Washington appreciated the unique opportunity it gave Theodore Roosevelt to aggressively pursue his conservation agenda. Roosevelt was never shy about using his executive powers, and the value of this important tool was quickly appreciated by his successors in both parties. This was much more than the government simply moving some small packets of land from one pocket to another. It gave Roosevelt an opportunity to invent a whole new type of pocket—a pocket in which to preserve America's heritage along with scientific and scenic wonders.

Arizona's national parks and monuments are spectacular national treasures. The effort 130 plus years ago to begin preserving these treasures changed the face of Arizona, in the sense that it allowed us to stop the relentless movement toward the disposal of our public lands and replaced it with a new focus on land stewardship and preservation. In Arizona, it has brought 20 national parks and monuments totaling more than 3,900,000 acres, or about 6,100 square miles. Arizona's national parks and monuments preserve much of what makes Arizona unique and much of what forms the centerpiece of our collective sense of place.

One

THE BEGINNING OF THE PRESERVATION MOVEMENT

Throughout much of the 19th century, the Southwestern portions of the United States were viewed as arid and desolate lands, potentially rich in natural resources but presenting immense challenges for settlement and economic development. Nearly all of the land was owned by the federal government, which was anxious to get it surveyed and eligible for disposal to the private sector. At the government level, minimal thought had been given to the preservation or protection of the natural wonders found throughout the Southwest, and even less to the preservation or protection of the artifacts of the cultures that had occupied these lands for millennia. The land was there to be exploited.

The impetus to challenge this view of the American Southwest did not come, for the most part, from the leaders of the government. It was a grassroots movement involving scientists and academics, as well as locals who had grown to appreciate the magnificent scenery and marvel at the structures and artifacts left by the earlier residents of the region. Eventually, the leaders in the government took notice, but it was neither a quick nor smooth process to challenge and convert that earlier worldview. America may have invented the idea of the national park, but it took time and effort to allow it to grow and flourish.

The years immediately following the conclusion of the Civil War saw a sharp increase in the number of immigrants and travelers to the American Southwest and specifically to the territories of Arizona and New Mexico. Many of these new arrivals marveled at the ruins of the prehistoric native settlements, such as Casa Grande, seen in this photograph from the early 1870s. (Courtesy of National Park Service.)

The stories and pictures from the early settlers excited the interest of ethnologists and archaeologists from major universities and museums. Prominent among them was Frederic W. Putnam, curator of the Peabody Museum of American Archaeology and Ethnology at Harvard, who, in 1879, published a beautifully illustrated book featuring the native ruins in Arizona and New Mexico, sparking even further interest. (Courtesy of National Institutes of Health.)

In 1879, the Archaeological Institute of America was founded and determined that its first field project should be a study of the Pueblo Indian ruins in Arizona and New Mexico. The Institute hired 40-year-old ethnologist Adolf Bandelier to lead this first archaeological investigation. (Courtesy of Project Gutenberg.)

In 1880, Bandelier traveled to New Mexico Territory and focused his investigations on the great pueblo ruins of Pecos, pictured here. Bandelier described Pecos as "probably the largest aboriginal structure within the United States, so far described" but then warned "in general the vandalism committed in this venerable relic of antiquity defies all description." (Courtesy of Library of Congress.)

Bandelier's reports on vandalism convinced the Archaeological Institute of America to seek Congressional help. Massachusetts senator George Frisbee Hoar was also a trustee of the Peabody Museum and a regent of the Smithsonian Institution. In 1882, Hoar petitioned the Senate to withhold from Land Office sale the properties containing these antiquities so that the ruins could be preserved. Unfortunately, Congress was not ready to act. (Courtesy of Library of Congress.)

The ruins at Casa Grande had been well known for nearly two centuries. Jesuit priest Eusebio Kino said Mass there in 1694, and visits to it had been reported numerous times in the 18th and 19th centuries. Its structures had visibly deteriorated during that period. This picture of tourists in 1888 shows the fragile condition of the main building. (Courtesy of National Park Service.)

The effort to protect Casa Grande was led by Boston philanthropist Mary Hemenway. In the late 1880s, she sponsored the Hemenway Southwestern Archeological Expedition, a multiyear study of Arizona Indian antiquities. In early 1889, under her leadership, Senator Hoar was persuaded to again ask Congress to protect Casa Grande, as it was "entirely unprotected from the depredations of visitors." (Courtesy of National Park Service.)

In March 1889, Congress approved an appropriation of $2,000 to repair and protect Casa Grande, and work began immediately. Although some of the damage was due to natural elements and simple vandalism, an increasing problem was posed by pothunters seeking to find and sell Indian artifacts, such as the pots from Casa Grande shown here, to collectors from around the world. (Courtesy of Library of Congress.)

On June 22, 1892, Pres. Benjamin Harrison signed an executive order acknowledging the archaeological value of the ruins and reserving 480 acres for the permanent protection of Casa Grande, making it the first national archaeological reservation in US history. (Courtesy of Library of Congress.)

During the early 1890s, public interest in American Indian antiquities grew very rapidly, thanks to photographs and exhibitions. The most prominent of these exhibitions was at the 1893 World's Columbian Exposition in Chicago. The state of Colorado sponsored a wildly popular cliff dwellers' pavilion at the fair, pictured here, which showcased the pots and other antiquities found at cliff dwellings in the American Southwest. (Courtesy of Project Gutenberg.)

The growing popularity of authentic Indian artifacts quickly reached across the Atlantic Ocean and caught the attention of Gustaf Nordenskiöld, part of a famous Swedish family of scientists and explorers. He decided in 1891 to explore and excavate, with local assistance, the pueblo ruins at Mesa Verde in Colorado. At that time, no permissions were required to excavate or remove antiquities. (Courtesy of National Park Service.)

Nordenskiöld took this picture of Mesa Verde's Cliff Palace Ruins in 1891. His excavation yielded a tremendous collection of artifacts that he catalogued, packed, and shipped back to Sweden. He produced a beautifully illustrated book about the artifacts he removed, many of which still remain in Finland's National Museum in Helsinki. This loss of American antiquities to a foreigner caused outrage among American archaeologists and ethnologists. (Courtesy of National Park Service.)

J. Walter Fewkes was the leader of the Hemenway Southwestern Archaeological Expedition in 1889 and supervised the renovations at Casa Grande. He became a leading expert on the variations of pottery amongst the prehistoric Southwestern Native Indians. He was also an early, strong voice to urge the protection and preservation of American antiquities. (Courtesy of Library of Congress.)

In 1896, Fewkes described in *American Anthropologist* his observations of the vandalism occurring at Palatki Ruins, pictured here, near Sedona, Arizona— "A commercial spirit is leading to careless excavations for objects to sell, and walls are ruthlessly overthrown, buildings torn down in hope of a few dollars' gain." Fewkes strongly believed that the time was right for meaningful preservation legislation. (Courtesy of Matthew Field, www.photography. mattfield.com Cc-by-sa-2.5.)

Edgar Lee Hewett was a young anthropologist who undertook extensive archaeological work on numerous sites in the Southwest. His commitment to the preservation effort and willingness to work within the federal political process made him a leader in the effort that eventually led to the passage of the Antiquities Act of 1906. (Courtesy of National Park Service.)

By the beginning of the 20th century, Chaco Canyon, with the Pueblo del Arroyo, had become a notorious pothunters' site with thousands of artifacts being unscientifically removed and taken out of state. Hewett had extensively worked Chaco Canyon, and in 1902, he guided Congressman John F. Lacey on a comprehensive tour of threatened antiquities sites in the Southwest. (Courtesy of Library of Congress.)

Lacey became committed to the preservation cause and was in a position to make things happen. As chairman of the House Committee on Public Lands, Lacey spent the next several years working with Hewett and others to draft and negotiate legislation allowing the president to set aside land containing prehistoric ruins and other items of scientific interest. In June 1906, Congress passed the Antiquities Act. (Courtesy of Library of Congress.)

The legislation authorized the president to proclaim the reservation of public lands containing "historic and prehistoric structures, and other objects of historic or scientific interest" as "national monuments." The size of these national monuments "shall be confined to the smallest area compatible with the proper care and management of the objects to be protected." Pres. Theodore Roosevelt signed the bill into law on June 8, 1906. (Courtesy of Library of Congress.)

Two

THEODORE ROOSEVELT AND THE ANTIQUITIES ACT

The passage of the Antiquities Act in June 1906 did not guarantee the preservation and protection of the natural and human heritage treasures found on public lands. The legislation was broadly written and provided few details on how it should be interpreted and implemented. What exactly was meant by "other objects of historic or scientific interest?" What was meant by "shall be confined to the smallest area compatible with the proper care and management of the objects to be protected?" Congress had given broad authority to the president to protect the American heritage, but what would the president do? What would future presidents do? What would happen if Congress did not like the way the Antiquities Act was being used? Would it work?

Of course, by June 1906, Congress had a fairly good idea of the style and personality of the current president, Theodore Roosevelt. After almost five years in office, Roosevelt's strength of personality, self-confidence, and enjoyment of power were well understood throughout the government and the American public. Equally well understood was Roosevelt's commitment to the concepts of conservation and preservation of natural resources. His love of the American West, of history, of birds, and big game were already the stuff of legends. Pres. Theodore Roosevelt would not hesitate to act, and act aggressively, in support of his beliefs. And act he did—proclaiming 18 national monuments over the remaining 33 months of his presidency, and quickly setting the precedent for aggressive and controversial use of the power of the Antiquities Act.

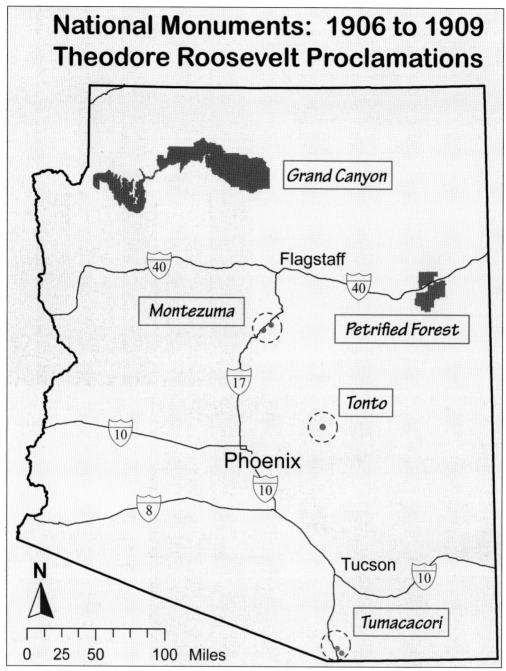

National Monuments: 1906 to 1909
Theodore Roosevelt Proclamations

Grand Canyon

Flagstaff

Montezuma

Petrified Forest

Tonto

Phoenix

Tucson

Tumacacori

N

0   25   50   100   Miles

Arizona's five national monuments proclaimed by Pres. Theodore Roosevelt are scattered throughout the state but are easily accessible to tourists. Perhaps the most "off the beaten path" is Tonto National Monument, located about two hours from Phoenix on state highway 188, just south of Roosevelt Lake. (Map by Donna Hartz.)

Theodore Roosevelt was a man who believed in action and believed in taking advantage of the powers of the presidency. When Congress put an end date on his ability to create national forests, he ordered the creation of 94 new national forests the day before the deadline. A confirmed preservationist, he determined to take maximum advantage of the powers given him by the Antiquities Act. (Courtesy of Library of Congress.)

Despite being born and raised in New York, Roosevelt was a man of the West, an outdoorsman, a hunter, and an accomplished naturalist. He was happy to sign the Antiquities Act of 1906 into law. During his presidency, he created 150 national forests, 51 federal bird reserves, 18 national monuments, 5 national parks, and 4 national game preserves. (Courtesy of Library of Congress.)

This 1892 photograph of Devils Tower in Wyoming shows the first national monument proclaimed under the Antiquities Act. Roosevelt's proclamation on September 24, 1906, cited Devils Tower as "an extraordinary example of the effect of erosion in the higher mountains as to be a natural wonder and an object of historic and great scientific interest." He already stretched the interpretation of the Act in his first proclamation. (Courtesy of Library of Congress.)

For his second national monument Roosevelt turned to the Southwest, proclaiming El Morro National Monument on December 8, 1906, and citing "the rocks known as El Morro and Inscription Rock . . . are of the greatest historical value." This photograph from 1873 shows the south side of the famous Inscription Rock. (Courtesy of US Geological Survey.)

For his third national monument proclamation, Roosevelt turned to Arizona. On December 8, 1906, he created Montezuma Castle National Monument, citing it as being of "the greatest ethnological value and scientific interest." This photograph of Montezuma Castle is from 1887. (Courtesy of Library of Congress.)

The cliff dwelling or "castle," as seen in this photograph from 1887, was built by the Sinaguan people, probably beginning about 1200 AD. They occupied the dwelling until the early 15th century. The soldiers and prospectors who visited these sites in the 1860s thought they had been built by the Aztecs, hence the name Montezuma Castle in recognition of the Aztec leader. (Courtesy of Library of Congress.)

Montezuma Well, seen in this 1886 photograph, is located about 11 miles from Montezuma Castle. It was formed by the collapse of a limestone cavern, and contains approximately 15 million gallons of water. Over one million gallons flow from springs into the lake every day, providing a valuable water resource for people and wildlife. Montezuma Well was added to the national monument in 1943. (Courtesy of Library of Congress.)

This photograph from 1886 shows an example of the dwellings in the limestone cliffs above Montezuma Well. These dwellings also date back to the Sinagua people, who farmed the surrounding land more than 700 years ago. The Sinagua constructed canals to irrigate their farms, and those same canals are still in use today. (Courtesy of Library of Congress.)

Arizona's Verde Valley attracted large numbers of prospectors, soldiers, and settlers during the last half of the 19th century. Publicity concerning the cliff dwelling sites and demands for artifacts resulted in extensive vandalism at Montezuma Castle. Archaeologists also flocked to the area to document and protect the sites and remove the vulnerable artifacts. This early photograph shows pottery in situ. (Courtesy of Library of Congress.)

In the early days of Montezuma Castle National Monument, visitors were allowed to freely roam throughout the ruins, and the cliff dwelling became a popular tourist attraction. Some visitors were careful, but others inadvertently damaged the structures or removed various souvenirs. This early photograph shows visitors on the top floor of the castle. (Courtesy of National Park Service.)

The main structure within the Montezuma Castle complex contained about 20 rooms, but more than 65 additional rooms were found in adjacent structures and along the cliffs. Archaeologists estimate that the Montezuma Castle complex could have housed as many as 150 people. This photograph from the 1930s shows the then-current status of the preservation effort. (Courtesy of National Park Service.)

Until 1951, the Montezuma Castle Ruins were fully accessible to casual visitors. This photograph from the 1940s shows the series of wooden ladders that visitors used to access the site. The potential dangers involved in having the public climb wooden ladders and the real damage the public inflicted on the structures necessitated a change in policy. (Courtesy of National Park Service.)

Various Works Progress Administration projects in the late 1930s significantly improved the visitor experience—improving the access roads and building structures to allow for the opening of a visitor center and museum. This photograph from the 1950s shows an outdoor exhibit area containing a model of the castle structure. (Courtesy of National Park Service.)

Montezuma Castle National Monument is now a major tourist attraction. The easy access from Interstate 17, a major north-south route in Arizona, enabled it to attract nearly one million annual visitors during the first decade of the 21st century. Many pose for photographs showcasing the results of more than a century of preservation efforts. (Courtesy of the Hartz family.)

President Roosevelt proclaimed Petrified Forest National Monument on December 8, 1906, the same day he also proclaimed Montezuma Castle National Monument. His proclamation cited "the mineralized remains of Mesozoic forests . . . are of the greatest scientific interest and value." This photograph from 1895 shows what was called the "Jasper Forest." (Courtesy of National Park Service.)

The existence of a vast area of petrified wood was first documented and publicized in the 1850s, attracting much curiosity and an inevitable array of treasure seekers, despite the difficulty in getting there. Many of the formations were vandalized by visitors. In 1895, Congress turned down a bill to create a national park to protect Petrified Forest, the same year this photograph was taken. (Courtesy of National Park Service.)

In 1904, the US Geological Survey sent an expedition to Petrified Forest to document its treasures and better understand the processes that resulted in the petrifaction of the trees. This photograph from 1904 shows a group of geographers standing on a bridge formed by a petrified tree trunk. (Courtesy of US Geological Survey.)

The Petrified Forest area contained much more than just the "mineralized remains of Mesozoic forests." Eons of erosion from storms and rivers shaped stunning rock formations as the region was uplifted during the formation of the Colorado Plateau. This photograph from 1904 shows a formation nicknamed "Ostrich Rock." (Courtesy of US Geological Survey.)

The turn of the 20th century saw a sharp increase in tourism to the region. Among the many visitors to Petrified Forest was famed naturalist John Muir, shown in this photograph from 1905. Muir and others continued to press for federal protection for this amazing landscape, culminating in Roosevelt's proclamation the following year. (Courtesy of National Park Service.)

The petrified logs and tree stumps that so fascinated the visitors resulted from trees knocked down by wind or water and buried by sediment before they could decompose. Nearby volcanoes deposited layers of ash, and groundwater dissolved silica from the ash, which then seeped into the cells of the logs and eventually crystallized as the mineral quartz. (Courtesy of National Park Service.)

Other minerals combined with the quartz to produce the wide array of colors found in the petrifaction process. Eventually erosion carried away the overlying sediment, exposing the petrified logs, such as this one, nicknamed "the Cannon," pictured in 1915. (Courtesy of US Geological Survey.)

The varying minerals in the layers of eroded rock produced the colorful effects reflected in the naming of the surrounding area as the Painted Desert. This photograph shows the popular "Eagles Nest" formation, which unfortunately collapsed after heavy storms in late January 1941. (Courtesy of National Park Service.)

Petrified Forest National Monument contains much more than just geologic wonders. The human history is rich and varied. A culture known as the "Basketmakers" lived in the area between 500 BC and 650 AD, producing beautiful basketry. The Puebloan Anasazi people occupied the area after about 900 AD. This petroglyph, known as "Jitterbug," is testimony to their artistic abilities. (Courtesy of National Park Service.)

Agate House, seen in this photograph, was produced by the Anasazi between 900 and 1200 AD from hundreds of pieces of petrified wood. During the 1930s, workers from the Civilian Conservation Corps reconstructed the Agate House under the guidance of archaeologists. (Courtesy of US Geological Survey.)

Petrified Forest also contains sites from more recent history. This photograph shows the ruins of a stage station. A part of the National Old Trails Road, established in 1912, passes through the area. Petrified Forest, upgraded to a national park in 1962, is also the only national park through which the historic Route 66 once passed. (Courtesy of National Park Service.)

Petrified Forest has always been a place of wonder. Visitors marvel at the "forest" of petrified trees, the beauty of the Painted Desert, the myriad of weird rock formations left by erosion, and the reminders of the peoples who once lived in this land. It will always be a place where the younger tourists can acquire their own petrified rock souvenirs. (Courtesy of Library of Congress.)

On December 19, 1907, President Roosevelt proclaimed Tonto National Monument, citing that "two prehistoric ruins of ancient cliff dwellings . . . are of great ethnologic, scientific and educational interest." This photograph shows the two caves containing the cliff dwellings. (Courtesy of National Park Service.)

The dwellings within these remote caves in the rugged Tonto Basin were built by a culture known as the Salado people. They occupied this area in the 13th, 14th, and early 15th centuries. They were farmers and fine artisans, making beautiful pottery and textiles. It is unknown why they began living in these cave dwellings, and why they disappeared by the mid-1400s. (Courtesy of National Park Service.)

The Lower Cliff Dwelling, seen in this 1905 photograph, contains 20 rooms. Construction was probably started about 1300. The cave containing the Lower Cliff Dwelling is about 40 feet high, 85 feet wide, and 48 feet deep. (Courtesy of National Park Service.)

The rooms in the Lower Cliff Dwelling were small. Although the rooms were heavily vandalized, visitors can see evidence of fire pits, mortar holes, and clay floors. The local stone was the primary building material, with pine and juniper used for roof beams. (Courtesy of National Park Service.)

The Upper Cliff Dwelling, seen in this 1920 photograph, was larger and situated in a much bigger cave. Its cave was 80 feet high, 70 feet wide, and 60 feet deep. The Upper Cliff Dwelling contained 40 rooms, and had enough space for a cistern capable of holding about 100 gallons of water. (Courtesy of National Park Service.)

Archaeological exploration of the Upper Cliff Dwelling has revealed middens containing mesquite beans and lima beans, and rooms containing pottery fragments, gravesites, baskets, basket fragments, and textile remnants. This photograph of the Upper Cliff Dwelling is from 1941. (Courtesy of National Park Service.)

The Tonto Basin remained sparsely occupied in the centuries after the disappearance of the Salado people. The first written record of the Tonto cliff dwellings is in an 1880 diary of local schoolteacher Angeline Brigham Mitchell. Vandals visited the site in the following decades, with tourists arriving by the beginning of the 20th century. This photograph shows the Tonto National Monument museum in 1938. (Courtesy of National Park Service.)

Despite its relatively remote location, Tonto National Monument remains a popular tourist destination. The monument offers a museum with video presentations, a short hike to the Lower Cliff Dwelling, a longer seasonal hike to the Upper Cliff Dwelling, and beautiful views across the basin to Roosevelt Lake, as seen here. (Courtesy of National Park Service.)

Tumacácori National Monument, shown in this 1870 photograph, was established September 15, 1908, by Theodore Roosevelt's proclamation to "preserve the (mission church) ruin with as much land as may be necessary for the protection thereof." Originally consisting of the mission and 10 acres, it was expanded twice. In 1990, Congress added two nearby Spanish missions, Guevavi and Calabazas, and changed Tumacácori's designation to Tumacácori National Historical Park. (Courtesy of Library of Congress.)

In 1687, Padre Eusebio Kino, a Jesuit missionary, arrived in the Pimería Alta (Land of the Upper Pimas), which is, in modern times, the area of southern Arizona and northern Sonora, Mexico. Padre Kino and the Jesuits established more than 20 missions to convert the native population. In 1691, mission San José de Tumacácori was established outside of an O'odham village located east of the Santa Cruz River. (Courtesy of Library of Congress.)

The missions are built of adobe bricks and lime plaster. Adobe, while amazingly resilient to the harsh environment of the desert, can also become quite fragile. Preservation efforts are critical to the missions. Expenditures for preservation are estimated at more than $20 million since the establishment of the national monument. These preservation efforts continue today, entailing about 1,000 man hours annually. (Courtesy of Library of Congress.)

As a mission, San Cayetano de Calabazas's life was short. The mission was probably established sometime around 1756, was half built by 1761, and was functional by 1773. Abandoned as a mission in 1786, Calabazas's subsequent uses included a farm to supply Tumacácori and, after it was sold, a ranch house, post office, customs house, and, briefly, as Fort Mason. By 1878, Calabazas was a roofless shell. (Courtesy of Library of Congress.)

The Guevavi mission, seen in this 1937 photograph, had a series of names in its lifetime. It was first named San Gabriel de Guevavi, then San Rafael and San Miguel de Guevavi. Eventually, it became more commonly known as Los Santos Ángeles de Guevavi. The ruins are of a second church built in 1751 and abandoned in 1775. It was added to Tumacácori National Historic Park in 1990. (Courtesy of Library of Congress.)

The exact meaning of "Tumacácori" is unknown, and may never be known, as translation of O'odham words into Spanish often proved difficult. The NPS website lists numerous ideas of its meaning, which vary considerably. These include: "place where the wild chiles [sic] are gathered," "place of the flat rock," "flat rocky place," and "caliche bend." (Courtesy of Library of Congress.)

Three

THE STRUGGLE TO PRESERVE THE GRAND CANYON

The Grand Canyon in Arizona is universally considered one of the wonders of the natural world. Along with Yellowstone and Yosemite, it is considered one of the "crown jewels" of the National Park Service. More than anything else, it is widely viewed as the symbol of Arizona. Surely, it would be one of the first and highest priority examples of enlightened preservation.

In 1864, Abraham Lincoln authorized the state of California to use federal land to create a state park protecting the wonders of the Yosemite Valley and the nearby Mariposa Big Tree Grove. In 1872, Congress and Pres. Ulysses Grant passed and signed legislation to designate Yellowstone as the first national park. One might expect that the Grand Canyon would quickly follow Yellowstone and Yosemite as national parks. However, Grand Canyon did not become a national park until 1919, although it was protected as a national monument in 1908.

During that period Congress was creating other national parks—in 1890 Sequoia, Yosemite, and General Grant National Parks; in 1899 Mount Ranier; in 1902 Crater Lake; in 1903 Wind Cave; in 1904 Sullys Hill; in 1906 Mesa Verde; in 1910 Glacier; in 1915 Rocky Mountain; in 1916 Lassen Volcanic; and in 1917 Mount McKinley National Park—and so, the Grand Canyon had to wait.

Even under the Antiquities Act, President Roosevelt proclaimed 10 other national monuments before getting to the Grand Canyon in 1908. This chapter tells the story of the creation of Grand Canyon National Monument, later National Park, and why it took so long and was so controversial.

After it became a national park in 1919, the Grand Canyon story remained complicated. In 1932, Pres. Herbert Hoover proclaimed a "new" Grand Canyon National Monument of 273,000 acres, which sat alongside Grand Canyon National Park until it was absorbed into the Grand Canyon National Park in 1975, along with the similarly adjoining Marble Canyon National Monument.

Despite its current status as one of the "crown jewels" of the National Park Service, Theodore Roosevelt's 1908 proclamation of Grand Canyon National Monument was extremely controversial, resulting in multiple legal challenges, which ended up delaying its designation as a national park until 1919. This view from the 1870 Wheeler Expedition is just the beginning of the story. (Courtesy of Library of Congress.)

1st Lt. George Wheeler led a series of expeditions to explore and map the land west of the 100th meridian. The goal of the Wheeler Survey was to produce detailed topographic maps. One of the lasting treasures from Wheeler's work is a series of photographs, such as this 1871 view of the Colorado River within the Grand Canyon. (Courtesy of US Geological Survey.)

John Wesley Powell in 1869 led his Powell Geographic Survey on a three-month exploration of the Colorado River through the Grand Canyon. This was the first known river passage through the canyon. In 1871–1872, Powell retraced his route with a second expedition, producing this 1872 image of the inner gorge. (Courtesy of US Geological Survey.)

Powell famously had a wooden armchair attached to his expedition boat. His boat was named the *Emma Dean*, in honor of his wife. This photograph from 1872 shows the *Emma Dean* within the Grand Canyon. (Courtesy of US Geological Survey.)

The Grand Canyon was created by the actions of the Colorado River and by erosion over a period of millions of years. The river within the canyon is 277 miles long, while the canyon itself is up to 18 miles wide and over a mile deep. This photograph from 1872 provides a glimpse of its grandeur. (Courtesy of Library of Congress.)

The depth and size of the Grand Canyon contains multiple climate zones and creates multiple major ecosystems. This results in estimated species counts of more than 1,500 plants, 355 birds, 89 mammals, 47 reptiles, 9 amphibians, and 17 fish. This inner gorge picture is from the 1872 Powell Expedition. (Courtesy of US Geological Survey.)

The Grand Canyon was not empty of human inhabitants during Powell's visits. Multiple Indian communities had lived in and visited the canyon for thousands of years. This photograph from 1873 shows John Wesley Powell with Southern Paiute chief Tau-Gu. (Courtesy of National Park Service.)

The Southern Paiutes traditionally occupied land north of the Colorado River. This 1873 photograph is of a Paiute woman. Evidence of human activity has been found in the canyon going back about 4,000 years. The Anasazi lived in and around the canyon for many centuries. In more recent centuries, the Havasupai, Hualapai, and Navajo communities are a part of the history within the Grand Canyon. (Courtesy of National Park Service.)

By the turn of the 20th century, the Grand Canyon was becoming a prime area for tourism. In 1901, the Atchison, Topeka & Santa Fe Railway completed a 71-mile rail line from Williams, Arizona, to the Grand Canyon rim for transport of both tourists and mining supplies and production. This 1901 photograph shows the first passenger train to the canyon. (Courtesy of National Park Service.)

Tourism quickly became the priority of the train to the Grand Canyon, as mining revenue was too unpredictable. Passengers on the mainline through northern Arizona could easily transfer at Williams and conveniently and comfortably see the wonders of the Grand Canyon. This 1905 photograph shows the train at the canyon station. (Courtesy of National Park Service.)

Pictures and stories of the Grand Canyon made it an important destination for those able to travel to the American Southwest. The views were spectacular, as was the thrill of walking along the canyon rim. This photograph from 1899 shows a tourist standing on the very edge of the rim. (Courtesy of National Park Service.)

Of course, the tourists wanted to see and experience more than just the views from the rim of the canyon. This photograph from 1906 shows a group of well-dressed tourists along the banks of the Colorado River at the bottom on the Grand Canyon. (Courtesy of Library of Congress.)

A visit into the depths of the Grand Canyon required a descent on one of several established trails. An early and popular option was the Bright Angel Trail. This photograph shows a mule train of tourists from 1909. Originally a Havasupai trail, it was improved, extended to the river, and managed by Ralph Cameron as a private business venture. (Courtesy of National Park Service.)

Mules have long been the preferred means of travel into the canyon. In 1887, John Hance probably became the first to advertise mule rides into the Grand Canyon down the Grandview Trail. As seen in this 1910 photograph, occasionally, the mules needed some encouragement. (Courtesy of National Park Service.)

The influx of tourists to the Grand Canyon at the turn of the 20th century meant a need for accommodations at the rim. By 1885, early tourism entrepreneur John Hance built a tent camp for tourists at Grandview Point. In 1905, the Atchison, Topeka & Santa Fe opened the elegant El Tovar Hotel in cooperation with the Fred Harvey Company, as seen in this 1905 photograph. (Courtesy of National Park Service.)

Of course, touring or working in the Grand Canyon sometimes was dangerous, and it remains potentially dangerous to this day. This photograph from 1906 shows a human skeleton found near the Bright Angel Trail. (Courtesy of National Park Service.)

The entrepreneurs at the Grand Canyon found numerous ways of making money from the tourists, in addition to selling transportation and accommodations. After a long hike or mule ride down the Bright Angel Trail, this photograph from 1905 shows what refreshments tourists found awaiting them in Bright Angel Canyon. (Courtesy of US Geological Survey.)

Perhaps the best way to "mine" the tourists was to charge tolls to use the trails—effectively, tolls to cross public lands. Ralph Cameron's control of the Bright Angel Trail enabled him to turn it into the Bright Angel Toll Road, as seen in this 1905 photograph. (Courtesy of National Park Service.)

It was becoming apparent to many that federal action would be required to curb the excesses of the miners and tourism entrepreneurs. On January 11, 1908, President Roosevelt proclaimed the Grand Canyon National Monument. 808,120 acres protecting "the greatest eroded canyon within the United States" were set aside, as seen in this 1908 photograph. This proclamation was controversial from the very beginning. (Courtesy of US Geological Survey.)

Roosevelt's proclamation promised to end or curtail several decades of private control of the canyon. A major opponent was one of the canyon's most aggressive businessmen, Ralph Cameron. He was a very powerful local politician and former sheriff, and with his brother Niles, he had extensive mining claims and had improved and controlled the Bright Angel Trail. (Courtesy of Library of Congress.)

As a national monument, the federal government had the right to end Cameron's extremely lucrative practice of charging tolls to use the Bright Angel Trail, the trail closest to the rim's tourism amenities. This photograph from 1906 shows Niles Cameron collecting tolls, a business that Ralph Cameron believed his mining claims allowed. (Courtesy of National Park Service.)

Ralph Cameron's ties to the Grand Canyon were extensive. This 1903 photograph shows one of his canyon camps. He was elected congressional delegate for Arizona Territory in 1908 and, later, used his election to the US Senate to oppose the Grand Canyon as a national monument and as a national park. He fought in court to regain his canyon property rights, finally losing in 1928. (Courtesy of US Geological Service.)

On February 26, 1919, Congress redesignated the Grand Canyon as a national park. The tourism facilities and National Park Service activities within the park expanded during the 1920s and 1930s. Seen in this 1934 photograph is a group of tourists guided by a park ranger along the Grandview Trail. (Courtesy of National Park Service.)

Grand Canyon National Park also benefited from the work of the Civilian Conservation Corps (CCC) during the 1930s, providing much needed manpower and funds for a wide range of improvements. This photograph from 1934 shows a CCC trail construction project within the park. (Courtesy of National Park Service.)

The northern rim of the Grand Canyon was much less accessible in the early years to prospectors, entrepreneurs, and tourists. There was no railroad access, and until Arizona became a state in 1912, Utah strongly believed that the land north of the Colorado River should belong to it. This 1929 photograph shows the Grand Canyon Lodge, which had opened on the north rim the previous year. (Courtesy of National Park Service.)

The north rim's Grand Canyon Lodge, designed by Gilbert Stanley Underwood, provided spectacular views of the canyon from both inside and outdoors on the large porch. The lodge was built by the Union Pacific Railroad, which ran bus tours to the north rim from Utah. (Courtesy of National Park Service.)

On September 1, 1932, a fire broke out in the kitchen of Grand Canyon Lodge and very quickly engulfed the entire structure. Everyone safely escaped, but the lodge was a total loss, as can be seen in this photograph from 1932. (Courtesy of National Park Service.)

It took nearly five years to rebuild the Grand Canyon Lodge. The basic floor plan remained the same, as did the spectacular views, but it was improved to better handle heavy snows and lessen the fire risk. This photograph from 1937 shows the new Grand Canyon Lodge nearing completion. (Courtesy of National Park Service.)

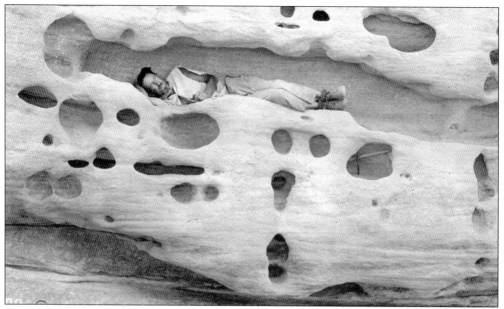

Grand Canyon National Park has always been a place where visitors can have fun and has been known for its scenery, geology, and history. One of the workers on a 1923 US Geological Survey of the park found a unique place to rest within the limestone cliffs of the canyon. (Courtesy of US Geological Survey.)

The size of Grand Canyon National Park has increased on several occasions since 1908, including the 1975 absorption of the second Grand Canyon National Monument. By 2013, it had grown to 1,217,403 acres, or 1,904 square miles. More than four million tourists visit the canyon each year, with most posing for pictures on the canyon rim. (Courtesy of the Hartz family.)

Four

THE BIRTH AND GROWTH OF THE NATIONAL PARK SERVICE

By the end of the Roosevelt administration in 1909, eighteen national monuments had been created including five in Arizona. Pres. William Howard Taft would add 10 more national monuments between 1909 and 1913. Unfortunately, the only real benefit to be realized from these Antiquities Act proclamations was protection of the land from disposal by the General Land Office. These proclamations included no money to staff these national monuments, nor any money for protection of threatened structures or artifacts, nor any money for creation or enhancement of any tourism infrastructure. The land could not be sold by the General Land Office, and that was about it.

The new national monuments also were not being "managed" in any consistent fashion. The president who proclaimed the national monument would decide to whom management responsibility would be assigned. Generally, it was assigned to whatever government department had previous responsibility for the land. Many national monuments were carved out of national forest reserves and were therefore managed by the Department of Agriculture. Others were managed by the Department of the Army or the Department of the Interior. The congressionally created national parks suffered from similar problems of inconsistent and, at times, unprofessional management, as well as chronic underfunding.

The period between the end of Theodore Roosevelt's presidency and the end of Franklin Roosevelt's presidency saw an explosion in the number of national monuments proclaimed under the Antiquities Act. Six presidents proclaimed 65 new national monuments, including 12 in Arizona. Plus Arizona gained another national monument through congressional action. In 1916, Congress created the National Park Service, which gradually took over responsibility for the professional management of these national monuments.

The period from the end of World War II until the start of the Clinton presidency saw the addition of only one national monument in Arizona but also saw the congressional redesignation of two of the monuments as national parks and the creation of a greatly expanded Grand Canyon National Park. This chapter tells these stories.

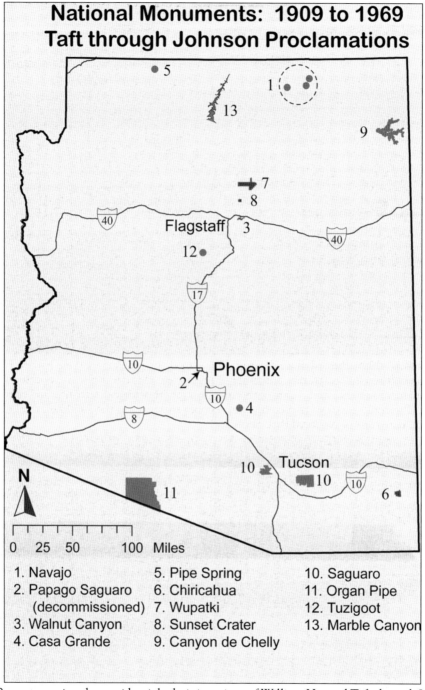

National Monuments: 1909 to 1969
Taft through Johnson Proclamations

• 5

1

13

9

7
• 8

Flagstaff 3

12•

Phoenix

2

• 4

Tucson
10 10 10

11 6

N

0	25	50		100	Miles

1. Navajo
2. Papago Saguaro
   (decommissioned)
3. Walnut Canyon
4. Casa Grande

5. Pipe Spring
6. Chiricahua
7. Wupatki
8. Sunset Crater
9. Canyon de Chelly

10. Saguaro
11. Organ Pipe
12. Tuzigoot
13. Marble Canyon

The 60 years covering the presidential administrations of William Howard Taft through Lyndon Johnson saw the addition of 13 new national monuments (not counting the second Grand Canyon National Monument), located throughout Arizona. This map shows the locations of those monuments. Several of these national monuments require some effort to reach, but visitors are well rewarded for their efforts with spectacular scenery and fascinating stories of the people who have inhabited this land. (Map by Donna Hartz.)

On March 20, 1909, Pres. William Howard Taft signed the proclamation for Navajo National Monument. It sought "to protect a number of prehistoric cliff dwellings and pueblo ruins . . . which are new to science and . . . are of the very greatest ethnological, scientific and educational interest." Protected are three non-contiguous sections surrounding the dwellings, totaling about 360 acres. (Courtesy of National Park Service.)

The monument, named for the Navajo Nation, whose land surrounds the monument, protects cliff dwellings occupied from about 1250 to 1300 AD. Keet Seel is seen in this photograph from the late 19th century. As with so many ancient dwellings in the Southwestern United States, Navajo National Monument's dwellings were being damaged by excavations, which were often done in search of sellable artifacts. (Courtesy of National Park Service.)

The people who built and lived in the dwellings are the ancestors of the local Native American peoples in the area—the Hopi, Navajo, Zuni, and San Juan Southern Paiute. Keet Seel and Betatakin are eight miles apart and were constructed mainly of stone blocks. About half of Inscription House was constructed of adobe blocks, and it is about 40 miles away. (Courtesy of National Park Service.)

Of the three, Betatakin is the best-preserved and is considered one of the premier dwellings in the Southwest. Its population likely peaked at 75 to 100 people. Though not all rooms remain, 135 rooms have been identified by archeologists. (Courtesy of National Park Service.)

Keet Seel is a Navajo name meaning "broken pottery scattered around." It is the largest dwelling in the monument and the earliest settled. Though no remnants remain of the earliest buildings, there is evidence of occupation in the local area by the year 950. Keet Seel was populated by about 150 residents at its peak. (Courtesy of National Park Service.)

Inscription House, seen in this photograph from 1909, is the smallest of the dwellings. It is also the most degraded because its rock overhangs are less protective than those of the other dwellings. It had been little visited due to inaccessibility, although roads built in the 1960s improved accessibility. The inability to stabilize the area in and around the ruins resulted in closure to the public in 1968. (Courtesy of National Park Service.)

Pres. Woodrow Wilson proclaimed Papago Saguaro a national monument on January 31, 1914, citing "splendid examples of the giant and many other species of cacti and the yucca palm . . . and that on the walls of the rocks among which these forms thrive best, there are numerous prehistoric pictographs of archaeological and ethnological value." Hole-in-the-Rock is seen in this early photograph of the Papago Buttes. (Courtesy of Scottsdale Public Library.)

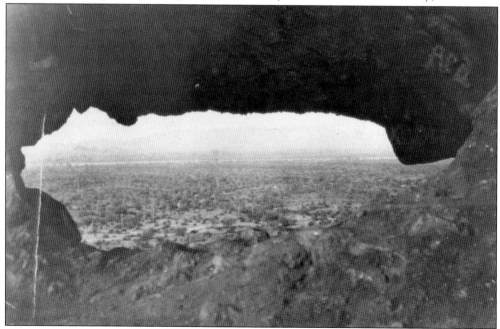

The Papago Buttes are sedimentary sandstone formations formed between six and fifteen million years ago that eroded over millions of years into the beautiful shapes and openings seen today. This early-20th-century view from Hole-in-the-Rock looks toward the then-small town of Phoenix, with a backdrop of South Mountain, the Estrella Mountains, and the White Tank Mountains. (Courtesy of Scottsdale Public Library.)

The Papago Saguaro area was a popular place for excursions by residents of the Phoenix area during the last decades of the 19th century. Picnics were extremely popular in the Hole-in-the-Rock formation, as seen here. Community leaders and citizens looked for ways to preserve this land for recreation in advance of it being opened for homesteading, leading to the proclamation by President Wilson. (Courtesy of Scottsdale Public Library.)

Even after the proclamation, there was pressure to use this land for a variety of purposes. This 1913 photograph shows a hydroelectric plant being built on the border of the monument. Requests were made to the federal government to approve roadways, expanded National Guard facilities, mining concessions, and so on. Tensions built over the proper use of these national monument lands. (Courtesy of Library of Congress.)

A request by Arizona in the 1920s to build a fish hatchery within the monument brought the situation to a head. Congressional legislation to return the land to Arizona was introduced in 1928 and 1929 and was finally signed into law on April 7, 1930. Papago Saguaro National Monument was no more, and the fish hatchery was built, as seen in this photograph from the 1930s. (Courtesy of Tempe History Museum.)

But Papago Park was born. Thanks to the CCC, the recreational facilities in Papago Park were greatly improved, and it became increasingly popular among Phoenix-area residents for picnicking, hiking, and relaxation. Four generations of the authors' families have enjoyed climbing Hole-in-the-Rock for the beautiful views, with youngsters enjoying posing for pictures as much in the early 21st century as they did in the late 19th century. (Courtesy of the Hartz family.)

During the brief lifespan of Papago Saguaro National Monument, many of the cactus and other desert flora that were cited in the proclamation had been badly vandalized. Concern grew among the citizenry, and in 1934, the Arizona Cactus and Native Flora Society was founded. By 1939, the society opened the Desert Botanical Garden in Papago Park, which remains one of the area's treasures. (Courtesy of Schilling Library, Desert Botanical Garden.)

Development plans for Papago Park in the 1950s included a golf course and a zoo. No public money was available for a zoo, so Robert Maytag agreed to lead a private development effort. The Arizona Zoological Society was founded, and in 1962, the Maytag Zoo was opened. Its name was changed to Phoenix Zoo in 1963 and it has expanded spectacularly since to take its place among America's great zoos. (Courtesy of Phoenix Zoo.)

Pres. Woodrow Wilson on November 30, 1915, proclaimed Walnut Canyon National Monument, preserving 1,879 acres. The original proclamation is neither poetic nor descriptive of the canyon or the ruins found within and states only that "certain prehistoric ruins of ancient cliff dwellings . . . are of great ethnologic, scientific and educational interest." (Courtesy of US Geological Survey.)

Walnut Canyon, seen in this photograph from the 1870s, is located on the pine-forested Colorado Plateau, east of Flagstaff. It consists of layers of sandstone and limestone that eroded to form natural alcoves and provides a natural water source in this otherwise dry land. Water drew both people and a large variety of wildlife to the canyon. (Courtesy of US Geological Survey.)

Access to water and the canyon's protective rock alcoves provided a prime location for numerous buildings and dwellings. Over 200 rock rooms still exist. Artifacts indicate that people passed through the area for several thousand years, and the canyon was occupied several times from about 600 to 1400 AD. The most intensive occupation occurred between 1000 and 1200 AD, when Walnut Canyon was home to 100 or more people. (Courtesy of US Geological Survey.)

Like so many of the ruins throughout the West, Walnut Canyon was under threat of complete destruction by pothunters and visitors looking for souvenirs to take home. The arrival of the railroad in the 1880s only increased the threat as visitors flocked to see these easily accessible ruins. (Courtesy of US Geological Survey.)

The CCC provided an important role in the preservation of Walnut Canyon. It stabilized ruins, constructed trails, and built a residence for employees and the original visitor center. Later expansions of the visitor center retained some of the original CCC building. (Courtesy of US Geological Survey.)

Original oversight was under the US Forest Service, but it was transferred to the National Parks Service in 1934. A second presidential proclamation on September 24, 1938, expanded Walnut Canyon National Monument to its current 3,579 acres. This photograph of Walnut Canyon is from the 1870s. (Courtesy of National Archives and Records Administration.)

The National Park Service was created in the Organic Act of 1916. Its first director was Stephen Mather. Its mission was "to conserve the scenery and the natural and historic objects and the wildlife therein and to provide for the enjoyment of the same in such manner and by such means as will leave them unimpaired for the enjoyment of future generations." (Courtesy of Library of Congress.)

In 1933, Pres. Franklin Roosevelt issued an executive order transferring to the National Park Service all the national monuments then administered by the Department of Agriculture, as well as all historic sites managed by the War Department. The new National Park Service promoted itself through posters, such as this one from the 1930s. (Courtesy of Library of Congress.)

On August 3, 1918, Pres. Woodrow Wilson proclaimed Casa Grande Ruins, as seen in this photograph from 1870, a national monument, citing the need for "the protection, preservation and care of the ruins of the ancient buildings and other objects of prehistoric interest thereon." But that was neither the beginning nor the end of the story. (Courtesy of Library of Congress.)

In 1889, Congress had authorized the expenditure of $2,000 to "repair and protect" the ruins at Casa Grande, and in 1892, Pres. Benjamin Harrison ordered that 480 acres surrounding Casa Grande buildings be "reserved for the protection of the Casa Grande ruin." This photograph from 1900 shows the result of these initial efforts of repair and protection. (Courtesy of National Park Service.)

In 1899, the federal custodian for the Casa Grande Ruins Reserve determined that a roof structure would be needed to protect the ruins from further deterioration. It took several years to prove his point, but in 1903, a further appropriation of $2,000 to construct a roof was approved. The roof, as seen in this photograph from 1915, was finished in September 1903. (Courtesy of National Park Service.)

Casa Grande Ruins became a national monument in 1918, two years after the creation of the National Park Service. Soon, it was apparent that a better roofing solution was needed, as a windstorm in 1930 blew off part of the 1903 roof. A new, stronger design was approved, and construction finished in December 1932, as seen in this photograph. (Courtesy of National Park Service.)

The archaeological record at Casa Grande shows activity at the site going back to about 500 AD. Approximately 60 archaeological sites have been documented, and it is believed that the main Casa Grande building was constructed around 1200 AD. This photograph from 1937 shows details of the wall construction. (Courtesy of Library of Congress.)

The Hohokam culture, which built the Casa Grande complex, conducted large-scale irrigated farming, and there is evidence they maintained far-ranging trade relationships. The exact purpose of the Casa Grande structure, seen in this 1937 photograph, remains unknown, and similarly unknown are the reasons for its abandonment around 1450 AD. (Courtesy of Library of Congress.)

Although the site was heavily plundered during the last decades of the 19th century, a variety of artifacts have been found within Casa Grande Ruins National Monument. This photograph shows turquoise jewelry and mosaics recovered at the national monument. (Courtesy of National Park Service.)

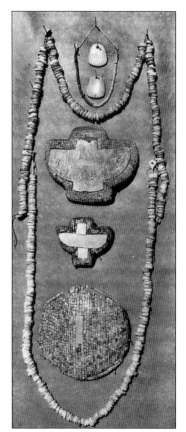

In addition to the personal or ceremonial decorative artifacts, archaeologists at Casa Grande Ruins National Monument have collected a wide range of more practical items, as seen in this photograph, used for hunting, food preparation, and so on. (Courtesy of National Park Service.)

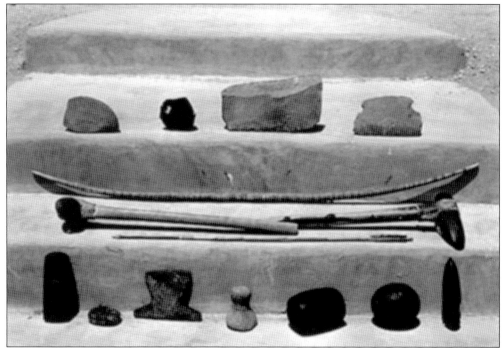

Pres. Warren G. Harding proclaimed Pipe Spring National Monument on May 31, 1923. It protects "a spring, known as Pipe Spring, which affords the only water along the road between Hurricane, Utah, and Fredonia, Arizona, a distance of 62 miles." This photograph of the east cabin is from the 1920s. (Courtesy of National Park Service.)

The monument is located on 40 acres in northern Arizona between the Grand Canyon and Zion National Parks. This important source of water drew people to it, with evidence of the Anasazi from about 1 AD. The Anasazi appear to have abandoned the area by about 1200 AD. (Courtesy of Library of Congress.)

Paiutes inhabited the area for three centuries prior to discovery by settlers of European descent. In 1858, the spring was found by a group of Mormons exploring the area, who then made efforts to protect and control the valuable water supply. In the late 1860s, the local Paiutes were joined by other nearby Indian tribes in attacking the Mormon settlement. (Courtesy of National Park Service.)

The Mormons responded by building a fortified sandstone house over the spring. In 1873, Anson Perry Winsor, the Mormon bishop of Grafton, Utah, was hired to manage the ranch and fort, which came to be known as "Winsor Castle," seen here. The ranch complex included two additional sandstones buildings—the east cabin and west cabin. (Courtesy of Library of Congress.)

In 1887, the Mormon Church lost ownership of Pipe Spring, though the ranch continued to be operated as a private ranch. This photograph from the 1930s shows the interior of Winsor Castle. In 1907, the Kaibab Paiute Indian Reservation was established, completely surrounding the 40-acre ranch. (Courtesy of Library of Congress.)

In 1923, the ranch was sold to the federal government to enable it to be protected by the proclamation to form the Pipe Spring National Monument. By that time, buildings were badly deteriorating, as seen in this photograph from the 1930s, and desperately needed the help of the National Park Service. (Courtesy of Library of Congress.)

During the 1930s, a Civilian Conservation Corps camp was established at the monument. The camp contained 13 buildings and a swimming pool. Among their projects, the CCC workers cleaned out the spring, built a new road through the monument, and graded the campground. (Courtesy of National Park Service.)

Current activities and exhibits at Pipe Spring include a well-rounded experience for visitors. The two cabins showcase historical ranching, and during the harvesting season, visitors can pick fruit from the orchards, which feature older heritage varieties. Exhibits and programs also focus on the culture and history of the Paiutes. (Courtesy of National Park Service.)

On April 18, 1924, Pres. Calvin Coolidge proclaimed Chiricahua National Monument, seen in this 1935 photograph, citing "certain natural formations, known as 'The Pinnacles,' within the Coronado National Forest, in the State of Arizona, are of scientific interest, and it appears that the public interests will be promoted by reserving as much land as may be necessary for the proper protection thereof, as a National Monument." (Courtesy of National Park Service)

Chiricahua National Monument originally consisted of 4,238 acres and was more than doubled in size through a proclamation by Pres. Franklin Roosevelt in 1938, with additional acreage added in 1978 and 1984. It currently totals 11,785 acres, 86 percent of which is further protected as federal wilderness. (Courtesy of National Park Service.)

The incredible geological formations are the result of millions of years of volcanic activity and constant erosion. The Chiricahua Mountains reach more than 9,700 feet in elevation and are about 40 miles long and 20 miles wide. "Punch and Judy," seen in this photograph, is one of the monument's most popular formations. (Courtesy of National Park Service.)

Another popular formation is "Balanced Rock," seen in this 1935 photograph. The Chiricahua mountain range is an example of what is called "sky islands." It is part of the Mandrean Archipelago, a series of nearby mountain groups, with the "sky islands" of mountains appearing in a line protruding from the surrounding "ocean" of desert land. (Courtesy of National Park Service.)

Chiricahua National Monument is also a place of great biodiversity. Two deserts (the Sonoran and the Chihuahuan) and two mountain ranges (the Rocky Mountains and Sierra Madre) all converge in this area, each contributing to the rich variety of flora and fauna found in the Chiricahuas. (Courtesy of National Park Service.)

This was also the longtime home of the Chiricahua Apaches. The Apaches called this area "the Land of Standing-Up Rocks" and, from the mid-19th century, began to actively resist American encroachment into their homeland. Led by Geronimo, seen here in 1887, they continued to defend their land until finally surrendering in 1886. (Courtesy of National Archives.)

In 1978, Congress added the 440-acre Faraway Ranch to Chiricahua National Monument. Swedish immigrants Neil and Emma Erickson homesteaded with a small cabin in 1886. In 1898, they expanded the cabin into a larger ranch house, which is seen in this snowy winter photograph. Neil Erickson became the first ranger for the Chiricahua Forest Reserve in 1903. (Courtesy of Library of Congress.)

The Ericksons' daughter Lillian married Ed Riggs in 1923, and they modernized and converted their home into the popular Faraway Ranch guest ranch, featuring horseback rides to see the geological wonders of Chiricahua National Monument. Faraway Ranch is listed in the National Register of Historic Places. (Courtesy of National Park Service.)

Pres. Calvin Coolidge proclaimed Wupatki National Monument on December 9, 1924. His proclamation cited "two groups of prehistoric ruins, built by the ancestors of a most picturesque tribe of Indians still surviving in the United States, the Hopi or People of Peace." This early view shows the main Wupatki Ruin and the ball court. (Courtesy of US Geological Survey.)

Wupatki National Monument consists of about 35,000 acres. The largest and best-preserved pueblo is known as Wupatki, seen in this recent photograph, but the monument also contains the remains of four other pueblos—Lomaki, Wukoki, Citadel, and Nalakihu. (Courtesy of the Hartz family.)

This 1930s photograph shows the ruins of the smaller Wukoki pueblo. Evidence has been found of human activity within the monument going back at least 10,000 years. In approximately 500 AD, the Sinagua peoples began building substantial structures in this area. (Courtesy of Library of Congress.)

The ruins of the Citadel pueblo are shown in this 1930s photograph. Although Sinagua means "without water," the Sinaguan society managed to survive as an agricultural culture. Without easy access to springs, they collected rainwater and managed to raise corn and squash. (Courtesy of Library of Congress.)

The large Wupatki pueblo was built during the early part of the 12th century. The eruption of Sunset Volcano during the previous century deposited cinders, which held water and aided agriculture. This led to a population increase throughout the region. Perhaps as many as 100 people lived in the Wupatki pueblo. (Courtesy of the Hartz family.)

The Wupatki pueblo, part of the interior of which can be seen in this 1930s photograph, was a multistory structure; in fact, Wupatki means "tall house" in the Hopi language. The pueblo contained about 100 rooms and was the largest structure within 50 miles. By 1225 AD, it was permanently abandoned. (Courtesy of Library of Congress.)

In addition to its pueblo structures, the Wupatki complex included what is believed to be a community center and a ball court. This photograph from the 1930s shows the ball court in the process of being excavated and restored. (Courtesy of Library of Congress.)

This photograph shows the fully excavated and restored Wupatki ball court. It was used for ceremonial games and likely also used as a meeting place for traders to display and exchange their goods. It is similar to those found in Meso-America and is the most northern example of this type of ball court. (Courtesy of National Park Service.)

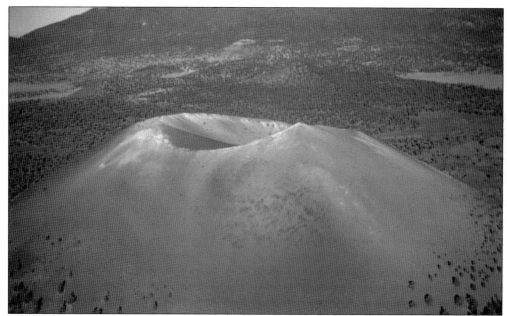

Sunset Crater National Monument was established by Pres. Herbert Hoover's proclamation on May 26, 1930, in response to a public outcry from the local community to protect the cinder cone known as Sunset Crater. The proclamation stated that "certain geologic formations . . . are of scientific and public interest, and . . . the proper protection of such formations appears to be desirable." (Courtesy of US Geological Survey.)

Local development pressures for mining, ranching, and logging provided the impetus to locals to try to save the monument. The tipping point to protect Sunset Crater came in 1928 when the film company for the movie *Avalanche* planned to dynamite Sunset Crater to film an actual avalanche. (Courtesy of US Geological Survey.)

Sunset Crater National Monument is 3,040 acres. The name was changed in 1990 to Sunset Crater Volcano National Monument. Sunset Crater is a 1,000-foot cinder cone. It is the youngest of the volcanoes in the San Francisco Volcano Field on the Colorado Plateau. (Courtesy of the Hartz family.)

Historically, this area was farmed prior to the volcanic eruption that occurred almost 1,000 years ago. Tree ring analyses dated the eruption to 1064, followed by about 200 years of volcanic activity in the area. However, recent research is questioning these dates. There is no evidence that anyone was caught in the eruption, but it is likely that residents relocated to places such as Walnut Canyon. (Courtesy of US Geological Survey.)

Legend claims the cinder cone was named by John Wesley Powell because the red and yellow colors surrounding the rim were the colors of the sunset. (Courtesy of US Geological Survey.)

Roads and hiking trails within the monument ring the cinder cone and provide access to some amazing volcanic features. The popular trail to the rim of Sunset Crater, however, was closed in 1973 due to damage from hikers. (Courtesy of US Geological Survey.)

Canyon de Chelly, seen in this 1873 photograph, is the only national monument in Arizona not created under the Antiquities Act. Creating the monument required a three-part cooperative effort. First, the Navajo Tribal Council Assembly adopted a resolution to allow creation of the national monument. Then an act of Congress authorized the presidential proclamation, which was then issued by Herbert Hoover on April 1, 1931. (Courtesy of Library of Congress.)

Canyon de Chelly, or Tseyi' in its Navajo name, which means "rock canyon," was heavily influenced by water. Flows of sediment-rich water, and sometimes flooding events, formed a rich, flat land that made the canyon an excellent location for settlement by ancient native people. Erosion-caused alcoves in the canyon walls provided ideal locations for dwellings. (Courtesy of US Geological Survey.)

The 1,000-foot rock walls of the canyons are mostly of pink cross-bedded de Chelly sandstone. Geologists believe the alcoves were created when water running through the canyon undercut sections of the sandstone. Freeze-thaw cycles and localized seeps weakened the cross-bedded rocks further, causing large sections to collapse. This erosion formed the curved recesses in the canyon where ancient native peoples built their homes. (Courtesy of Library of Congress.)

Often photographed, the majestic 800-foot spire Spider Rock sits at the junction between Canyon de Chelly and Monument Canyon. According to traditional Navajo beliefs, the taller of the two spires is the home of Spider Grandmother, one of the Holy Ones, who taught her people to weave and who spun her web of the universe. (Courtesy of US Geological Survey.)

There is evidence of several hundred inhabited sites within the canyon, spanning about 1,800 years. Evidence of farming in the area occurred much before the earliest permanent, round pit houses were built in about 500 AD. These earliest people are commonly referred to as the Basketmakers because they made and used baskets rather than pottery. (Courtesy of Library of Congress.)

The people living in the canyon in the 700s began to build stone, rectangular, and multistoried villages. These people are referred to as Ancient Puebloans or Anasazi. The White House Ruins, as seen in this photograph, were built between about 1100 and 1300 AD and are among the largest and most elaborate in the canyon. An extensive drought in the 1200s forced abandonment, although the canyon continued to be used periodically until modern times. (Courtesy of National Park Service.)

The White House Ruins, located close to the mouth of the canyon, are the most extensive and well preserved. There are two sections, with dwellings in the upper section and a lower ruin. The upper ruins are thought to be older and built around 1000 AD. There are about 60 rooms and 4 kivas (round ceremonial rooms) within the village. (Courtesy of Library of Congress.)

Antelope House, seen in this photograph from 1907, was named for the Navajo drawings of four antelopes found on its walls. It is the largest ruin located in the Canyon del Muerto section of Canyon de Chelly National Monument. It has been occupied by the Basketmakers from around 500 AD through to modern Navajo peoples. (Courtesy of Library of Congress.)

Mummy Cave Ruins, as seen in this photograph, were occupied from about 300 to 1300 AD and are located deep within Canyon del Muerto. The site takes its name from two mummified bodies found by archaeologists in the late 19th century. Its structures were built at various times throughout its history, and its most notable feature is a three-story tower. (Courtesy of Library of Congress.)

The Navajo retained ownership of the monument's land, seen in this 1904 photograph, with agreement for a "partnership to manage this special place." Congress charged the National Park Service with responsibility for administering the national monument, building roads, and maintaining visitor facilities. Visitors can hike to White House Ruins and drive the scenic rim roads, but direct backcountry access requires a permit and a Navajo guide. (Courtesy of Library of Congress.)

Pres. Herbert Hoover proclaimed Saguaro National Monument on March 1, 1933, as seen in this photograph from 1935. The proclamation protected 53,510 acres east of Tucson "because of the exceptional growth thereon of various species of cacti, including the so-called giant cactus." (Courtesy of US Geological Survey.)

The saguaro is native to the Sonoran Desert of southern Arizona and northern Mexico and is one of Arizona's quintessential, highly recognizable symbols. The late-spring white blossoms produce a fruit about half the size of a fist. The fruit was critical to the survival of native populations and continues to be important to local wildlife. It splits open to show its highly visible bright-red interior. (Courtesy of National Park Service.)

Throughout the area, these giants were threatened, shot up for target practice, and dug up for transplantation to private properties at an alarming rate. A second proclamation by Pres. John F. Kennedy on November 15, 1961, added 15,360 acres to the monument west of Tucson. This area is known as the Tucson Mountains District and was the backdrop of many mid-20th-century Western movies. (Courtesy of National Archives and Records Administration.)

These two distinct monument districts encompass a wide range of elevations, which result in multiple climate zones and ecosystems. They provide protected habitat for a large number of native plants and animals. It is estimated that the monument is home to over 1,200 species in the eastern Rincon Mountain District and about 400 species in the western Tucson Mountain District. (Courtesy of the Hartz family.)

Though slow growing, the saguaro cactus population census has shown a dramatic increase in the past several decades. The eastern Rincon Mountain District has experienced a 60-percent increase since 1990 and, in the western Tucson Mountain District, an increase of more than 67 percent. The 2010 census estimated there are 1,896,000 saguaro within the park. (Courtesy of National Park Service.)

Petroglyphs, or native prehistoric rock art, exist in many locations throughout the park and are evidence of long occupation by native populations. It is thought that Archaic peoples were in the area as far back as 5000 BC. The more recent Hohokam lived in the area from about 300 to 1450 AD, producing the petroglyph seen in this photograph. (Courtesy of National Park Service.)

Pres. Franklin Roosevelt proclaimed Organ Pipe Cactus National Monument on April 13, 1937. The proclamation cited that the Organ Pipe lands "contain historic landmarks, and have situated thereon various objects of historic and scientific interest." This photograph shows the organ pipe cactus, after which the monument is named. (Courtesy of National Park Service.)

Organ Pipe Cactus National Monument consists of 330,690 acres immediately north of the Mexican border. The monument maintains a "sister park" relationship with its Mexican neighbor, El Pinacate y Gran Desierto de Altar. This photograph shows a view of the monument landscape and cactus varieties. (Courtesy of National Park Service.)

The monument contains the only large stands of organ pipe cacti in the United States. This cactus, as seen in this photograph, can live for up to 150 years and produces its first flowers and fruit at about 35 years of age. The average height of a mature organ pipe cactus is 15 feet. (Courtesy of National Park Service.)

The land that is now Organ Pipe Cactus National Monument was long occupied by Indian, Spanish, and Mexican peoples. Prospecting and mining by Americans began in the late 19th century and ranching in the early 20th century. Initially, the local residents objected to the proclamation and the restrictions on the use of the land. (Courtesy of Library of Congress.)

The Gray family dominated the cattle ranching business during the 20th century. They secured water rights in 1919 and operated ranches, wells, and camps throughout the monument area, as seen in this photograph from the 1930s. (Courtesy of Library of Congress.)

The Dos Lomitas Ranch House, seen in this photograph, was the headquarters of the Gray family business. Its traditional style had thick adobe walls and a flat beamed ceiling. The last of the Gray family died in 1976, ending ranching within Organ Pipe Cactus National Monument. (Courtesy of National Park Service.)

Pres. Franklin Roosevelt proclaimed Tuzigoot National Monument on July 25, 1939. President Roosevelt cited that Tuzigoot had "situated thereon historic and prehistoric structures and other objects of historic or scientific interest." This photograph shows some of the walls and the Tower Room structure. (Courtesy of National Park Service.)

Construction at Tuzigoot began around 1000 AD by a pueblo-building culture known as the Sinagua people. They were farmers who stayed in the area for about 400 years. Tuzigoot was excavated between 1933 and 1935, as seen in this 1934 photograph of the excavation work. An Apache worker gave the site its name, which translates to "crooked water." (Courtesy of National Park Service.)

The Tuzigoot excavation project was supervised by two graduate students from the University of Arizona and funded by Franklin Roosevelt's Works Progress Administration and Civil Works Administration. This 1934 photograph shows workers thatching the roof of the Tower Room. (Courtesy of National Park Service.)

While local men were hired for excavation work, local women were assigned the responsibility of cleaning, sorting, and repairing the pots and other artifacts found during the excavation. This 1934 photograph shows the pottery workshop in nearby Clarkdale, Arizona. (Courtesy of National Park Service.)

The Tuzigoot pueblo has been estimated to contain 110 rooms in two- and three-story structures. The national monument itself is only 58 acres, but the total size of the preserved Tuzigoot complex is 834 acres. This photograph shows a portion of the restored pueblo. (Courtesy of National Park Service.)

Tuzigoot National Monument has remained extremely popular with visitors, and provides one of the best opportunities to experience a Sinaguan pueblo. It is visited by more than 100,000 people each year. (Courtesy of National Park Service.)

Pres. Lyndon Johnson proclaimed Marble Canyon National Monument on January 20, 1969. He cited Marble Canyon, seen in this photograph from the 1872 Wheeler Expedition, as "a northerly continuation of the world-renowned Grand Canyon, [which] possesses unusual geologic and paleontologic features and objects and other scientific and natural values." (Courtesy of Library of Congress.)

John Wesley Powell also explored Marble Canyon in 1872 on his way down the Colorado River to the Grand Canyon, as seen in this photograph from his survey. Powell chose the name Marble Canyon, although he knew, as a geologist, that the canyon walls were not made of marble. He believed that the polished limestone walls gave the appearance of marble. (Courtesy of US Geological Survey.)

This period also witnessed two other Arizona national monuments becoming Arizona's second and third national parks. On December 9, 1962, Congress redesignated Petrified Forest as a national park. This photograph shows the beautiful petrified wood and rock formations. (Courtesy of National Park Service.)

Since Herbert Hoover's proclamation of Saguaro National Monument in 1933, it was enlarged by more than 25 percent by a proclamation from President Kennedy in 1961. Congress redesignated it as Arizona's third national park on October 12, 1994, as seen in this spectacular saguaro forest view. (Courtesy of the Hartz family.)

Five

BILL CLINTON AND THE
NATIONAL LANDSCAPE
CONSERVATION SYSTEM

By the start of the Clinton Administration in 1993, 12 presidents had proclaimed 104 national monuments (Theodore Roosevelt with 18; William Howard Taft, 10; Woodrow Wilson, 14; Warren Harding, 8; Calvin Coolidge, 13; Herbert Hoover, 9; Franklin Roosevelt, 11; Harry Truman, 1; Dwight Eisenhower, 2; John Kennedy, 2; Lyndon Johnson, 1; and Jimmy Carter, 15). Republican and Democratic presidents had been similarly active in proclaiming monuments—60 by Republicans and 44 by Democrats. Only Republican presidents Richard Nixon, Gerald Ford, Ronald Reagan, and George H.W. Bush had not used the power of the Antiquities Act.

All of Carter's proclamations were in Alaska, where he used the Antiquities Act to protect sensitive pristine land from impending exploitation of natural resources, primarily energy resources. Excluding this special circumstance in Alaska, the Antiquities Act had been used only six times in the 50 years preceding the Clinton Administration. Things dramatically changed under Clinton and his secretary of the interior, Arizona's Bruce Babbitt, with 18 new monuments proclaimed, including five very large monuments in Arizona.

Clinton's renewed example of aggressive use of the Antiquities Act has been followed by his successors. Pres. George W. Bush proclaimed six monuments, five of which were marine monuments—with Hawaii's Papahanaumokuakea National Monument of 139,000 square miles the biggest monument ever proclaimed—more than all the other national parks and monuments combined. Pres. Barack Obama, through September 2013, had already proclaimed nine national monuments. There undoubtedly will be more to come during the Obama administration, maybe even in Arizona. Organized groups are pushing for three new national monuments in Arizona—Grand Canyon Watershed National Monument, consisting of 1.7 million acres; a 500,000-acre Northwest Sonoran Desert National Monument; and a Great Bend of the Gila National Monument of about 84,000 acres. After 107 years, the Antiquities Act of 1906 is still going strong and still controversial.

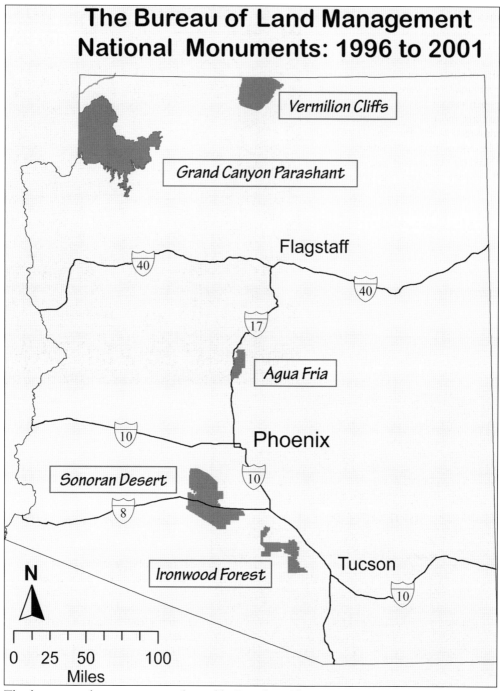

The Bureau of Land Management National Monuments: 1996 to 2001

Vermilion Cliffs

Grand Canyon Parashant

Flagstaff

40

40

17

Agua Fria

10

Phoenix

Sonoran Desert

10

8

Ironwood Forest

Tucson

10

N

0   25   50   100
        Miles

The five national monuments proclaimed by President Clinton in Arizona were huge, as can be seen in this map. They total approximately 2,015,000 acres, or more than 3,100 square miles. Agua Fria and Sonoran Desert National Monuments straddle interstate highways, through which millions traverse every year. Yet these monuments are little visited and little known. (Map by Donna Hartz.)

Pres. Bill Clinton used the authority of the Antiquities Act to create 18 new national monuments, and to expand the size of three others. Several of his proclamations were initially highly controversial, as was his decision to have most of the monuments managed by the Bureau of Land Management (BLM), rather than the National Park Service. (Courtesy of Library of Congress.)

Bruce Babbitt was President Clinton's secretary of the interior, a former governor of Arizona, and an ardent conservationist. Under Babbitt's leadership, the National Landscape Conservation System (NLCS) was established in 2000 within the BLM with a charge to "conserve, protect, and restore these nationally significant landscapes that have outstanding cultural, ecological, and scientific values for the benefit of current and future generations." (Courtesy of the Bureau of Land Management.)

The NLCS had been created without congressional action, so its existence would be at the whim of future presidents. To eliminate that risk, on March 30, 2009, Pres. Barack Obama signed into law the Omnibus Public Land Management Act of 2009, which congressionally established the BLM's National Landscape Conservation System. By 2013, it included 60 sites in Arizona alone. (Courtesy of Department of Interior.)

Though not in Arizona, the first national monument assigned to the Bureau of Land Management was the 1.9 million-acre Grand Staircase–Escalante in southern Utah. It was proclaimed on September 18, 1996, and was extremely controversial because of its massive size and Clinton's resurrection of the Antiquities Act. This 1944 photograph is of the Gothic Arch within Grand Staircase–Escalante. (Courtesy of US Geological Survey.)

On January 11, 2000, Clinton proclaimed Agua Fria National Monument to be managed by the BLM. The proclamation cited "an extraordinary array of scientific and historic resources. The ancient ruins within the monument, with their breathtaking vistas and spectacular petroglyphs, provide a link to the past, offering insights into the lives of the peoples who once inhabited this part of the desert Southwest." (Courtesy of the Bureau of Land Management.)

Agua Fria National Monument consists of 71,100 acres and is a relatively short drive north of Phoenix. It is named for the Agua Fria River, which cuts a canyon through the monument and provides a rich habitat for plants and animals. Elevations range from about 2,150 feet along the canyon floor to over 4,600 feet. (Courtesy of the Bureau of Land Management.)

The monument contains at least 450 prehistoric sites, with evidence of occupation spanning around 2,000 years. Between 1250 and 1450 AD, a pueblo culture thrived within the monument lands, with a population estimated at more than 3,000. Beautiful petroglyph sites are found throughout the monument. (Courtesy of the Bureau of Land Management.)

During the 19th century, settlers moving into the area encountered communities of Yavapai Indians maintaining a hunting and agricultural lifestyle. In the 1870s, the US Army forced the Yavapai into the San Carlos Reservation in eastern Arizona. The new settlers established cattle and sheep ranches. (Courtesy of the Bureau of Land Management.)

As a national monument managed by the Bureau of Land Management, permits for livestock grazing continue to be issued within the monument. Also, rights-of-way permits remain in place, but the activities are managed and controlled to limit environmental damage. (Courtesy of the Bureau of Land Management.)

In the mid- to late 19th century, prospectors scoured the area now covered by the national monument. Today, no new mining claims are allowed, but evidence of past mining activity can be found throughout the monument. This photograph shows the remains of the Richinbar Mine site. (Courtesy of the Bureau of Land Management.)

On January 11, 2000, President Clinton proclaimed Grand Canyon–Parashant National Monument to be jointly administered by the Bureau of Land Management and the National Park Service. It cited the new monument as "a vast, biologically diverse, impressive landscape encompassing an array of scientific and historic objects . . . The monument is a geological treasure." (Courtesy of the Bureau of Land Management.)

Grand Canyon–Parashant is located to the northwest of Grand Canyon National Park. It encompasses 1,048,321 acres of wild and beautiful landscape, as seen in this photograph. However, it also contains no visitor services, nor any paved roads. Amazingly, only five percent of the monument has even been surveyed. (Courtesy of the Bureau of Land Management.)

Human history in Grand Canyon–Parashant goes back some 13,000 years. The extent of the prehistoric artifacts remains unknown, although evidence of Archaic, Puebloan/Anasazi, and Southern Paiute cultures has been found. In modern times, mining and ranching activities began in the 1870s, leaving evidence of structures such as those seen in this photograph. (Courtesy of the Bureau of Land Management.)

During the first half of the 20th century, there were successful copper mining and smelting ventures within what is now Grand Canyon–Parashant National Monument. They left behind a variety of deteriorating structures and artifacts. This photograph from the BLM shows an example of ruins within the monument. (Courtesy of the Bureau of Land Management.)

A small, rough airstrip is located near the abandoned Grand Gulch copper mine within Grand Canyon–Parashant. The copper mine began in the 1870s and is on 20 acres of private land within the monument. The airstrip was scraped out in the 1930s and has crossing runways of 2,500 feet and 2,000 feet. There are no services at the airstrip. (Courtesy of the Bureau of Land Management.)

Grand Canyon–Parashant National Monument provides both challenges and opportunities for the potential visitor. There are beautiful natural and geological sights and camping opportunities, but only two semi-maintained hiking trails and no paved roads. (Courtesy of the Bureau of Land Management.)

President Clinton proclaimed Ironwood Forest National Monument on June 9, 2000, to be managed within BLM's new National Landscape Conservation System. The proclamation cited its "quintessential view of the Sonoran Desert with ancient legume and cactus forests" and noted that "the area holds abundant rock art sites and other archeological objects of scientific interest." (Courtesy of the Bureau of Land Management.)

One of the highlights of Ironwood Forest is the imposing Ragged Top Mountain. President Clinton's proclamation described it as "a biological and geological crown jewel amid the depositional plains in the monument." (Courtesy of the Bureau of Land Management.)

The 129,000-acre Ironwood Forest National Monument has a wide variety of terrain, with elevations ranging from 1,800 to 4,200 feet. It has primitive camping facilities, as well as opportunities for hiking, mountain biking, hunting, bird watching, wildflower viewing, and archeological sightseeing. (Courtesy of the Bureau of Land Management.)

As a national monument, Ironwood Forest is managed for multiple uses, including recreation and low-intensity cattle grazing. New mining claims are prohibited, as well as grazing of domesticated sheep and goats. The vandalized sign in this photograph warns of a high-pressure gas line. (Courtesy of the Bureau of Land Management.)

Evidence of human activity within Ironwood Forest National Monument goes back more than 5,000 years. Although most of the monument has not been surveyed, more than 200 Hohokam sites have been identified, from the period of 600 to 1400 AD. The Cocoraque Archaeological District contains numerous artifacts, as seen in this mound of petroglyphs. (Courtesy of the Bureau of Land Management.)

Ironwood Forest National Monument is extremely rich in petroglyphs from both the Archaic and Hohokam periods. The petroglyphs, as seen in this Cocoraque site photograph, contain human, animal, and geometric images. (Courtesy of the Bureau of Land Management.)

President Clinton proclaimed Vermilion Cliffs National Monument on November 9, 2000, assigning its management to BLM's National Landscape Conservation System. The proclamation cited Vermilion Cliffs as a "geological treasure" and recognized it as "Full of natural splendor and a sense of solitude, this area remains remote and unspoiled, qualities that are essential to the protection of the scientific and historic objects it contains." (Courtesy of the Bureau of Land Management.)

The area of the Vermilion Cliffs has been explored by numerous historic expeditions—in 1776 by the Dominguez-Escalante Expedition, in 1829 by the Antonio Armijo Mexican trading expedition, numerous Mormon exploring groups, and the Wheeler Expedition, which took this photograph in 1872. (Courtesy of Library of Congress.)

The monument is located on the high plateau to the north of the Colorado River, just south of Utah's Grand Staircase–Escalante National Monument. This photograph from 1923 shows the Vermilion Cliffs from Lee's Ferry. Vermilion Cliffs National Monument encompasses 293,000 acres. (Courtesy of US Geological Survey.)

Elevations within the monument range from 3,100 to 6,500 feet, exposing more than 3,000 feet of cliff face. The exposed layers of sandstone have long been of interest to geologists interpreting the natural and geological history of the area and are seen in this 1944 photograph from the US Geological Survey. (Courtesy of US Geological Survey.)

Visitors to Vermilion Cliffs National Monument have access to numerous spectacular scenic drives and hikes. There are an estimated 75 California condors in the monument, and condor-viewing sites are accessible. Many of the hikes require permits, and visitor information can be accessed at the Paria Contact Station. (Courtesy of the Bureau of Land Management.)

One of the scenic wonders within Vermilion Cliffs National Monument is the Canyon Buttes area. These formations were described in President Clinton's proclamation as "a geologically spectacular area where cross beds of the Navajo Sandstone exhibit colorful banding in surreal hues of yellow, orange, pink, and red caused by the precipitation of manganese, iron, and other oxides." (Courtesy of the Bureau of Land Management, photograph by Bob Wick.)

President Clinton proclaimed Sonoran Desert National Monument on January 17, 2001. The proclamation cited it as "a magnificent example of untrammeled Sonoran desert landscape" with "a spectacular diversity of plant and animal species" and "many significant archaeological and historic sites, including rock art sites, lithic quarries, and scattered artifacts." (Courtesy of the Hartz family.)

The 486,000-acre Sonoran Desert National Monument straddles numerous historic trails along the Southern Overland Route, including Indian trails, Spanish trails, pioneer trails, and the Butterfield Stage route. These trails provide numerous hiking and photography opportunities. (Courtesy of the Hartz family.)

Tom Childs operated the Papago Indian Chief copper mine smelter during the early decades of the 20th century. Unlike most small mines in Arizona, the Papago Indian Chief Mine had its own smelter, seen here. (Courtesy of Friends of the Sonoran Desert National Monument.)

Among the great diversity of flora and fauna within Sonoran Desert National Monument is the endangered subspecies the Sonoran pronghorn antelope. Although well adapted for arid conditions, it faces ongoing threats from climate change and drought, as well as human interference, including nearby military aviation activities. (Courtesy of John Hervert.)

INDEX

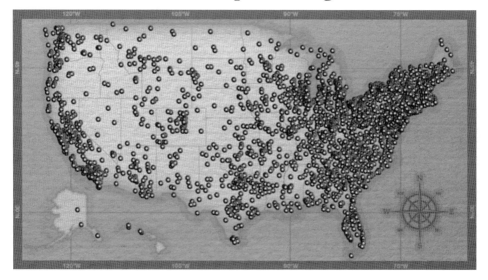